Echoes of the Soul

A Poetic Journey of Self-Discovering

Anne Melelita Brown

For Michelle

Copyright 2025 by Anne Melelita Brown

All rights reserved.

No portion of this book may be reproduced in any form without written permission from the publisher or author, except as permitted by U.S. copyright law.

This publication is designed to provide accurate and authoritative information in regard to the subject matter covered. It is sold with the understanding that neither the author nor the publisher is engaged in rendering legal, investment, accounting or other professional services. While the publisher and author have used their best efforts in preparing this book, they make no representations or warranties with respect to the accuracy or completeness of the contents of this book and specifically disclaim any implied warranties of merchantability or fitness for a particular purpose. No warranty may be created or extended by sales representatives or written sales materials. The advice and strategies contained herein may not be suitable for your situation. You should consult with a professional when appropriate. Neither the publisher nor the author shall be liable for any loss of profit or any other commercial damages, including but not limited to special, incidental, consequential, personal, or other damages.

Book Cover by Tukotuku Publishing

Illustrations by Tukotuku Publishing

First edition 2025

Print ISBN: 978-1-991366-91-7

Ebook ISBN: 978-1-991366-92-4

Contents

Echoes of The Soul	1
A Poetic Journey of Self-Discovery	
I am Okay Today	4
Sound of Truth	5
Waiting Game	6
Christopher	8
Discovery	10
Uncertainy	12
My Forever Man	14
One Wish	16
My Man	17
Embark on Another Adventure	19
Tears That Fall Suddenly	21
A Moment Feeling	23

Resolving Past Issues	25
Safety Boundaries	27
Who am I?	29
The Beach	31
Ray of Sunshine	32
Moving Forward	34
Strength	36
The Fight for Love	38
Hurtful Words	40
Easiest Way Out	42
Mother	44
Twin Flame	46
Ones Needs	48
Who Are You	49
Marriage to You	51
Ones Confidence	53
Through My Eyes	55
Life's Uncertainties	57
Better Within	59
Guiding Hand	61
Today Is Another Day	63
Look Within	64

For So Long	65
Would Like To Happen	66
Anne Melelita is Very Happy	68
Silent Whispers	69
Peace and Love	71
Reflection and an Invitation	72
Meet Anne Melelita	74

Echoes of The Soul

A Poetic Journey of Self-Discovery

Anne Melelita Brown's poetry captures the essence of life's ebb and flow, each piece a deep dive into the tumultuous journey of self-discovery and spiritual awakening. Her work is a delicate tapestry woven from her experiences, guiding readers through a maze of emotions and moments that define the human experience. As a poet from the verdant landscapes of New Zealand, her gentle, loving nature shines through each line, offering solace and understanding to anyone navigating their own path toward inner peace.

The collection begins with "I am Okay Today," a poignant reflection on the inevitability of change and the choices it forces us to make. Through her verse, Anne Melelita explores the human instinct to either flee from change or to confront it head-on. This theme of choice and acceptance is a recurrent one, echoing throughout her works as she delves into personal transformation against the backdrop of everyday life.

In "Sound of Truth," Anne Melelita confronts the stark realities of her past—moving houses 69 times and the transient relationships that marked her early years. Her journey from flight to fight, from a life of avoidance to one of confrontation, is laid bare, encapsulating a powerful moment of realization in "fight or flight," where she chooses to stand firm and embrace her true self.

The struggle with internal chaos and the quest for clarity are beautifully rendered in poems like "Resolving Past Issues" Here, Anne Melelita articulates the fog of confusion that clouds one's vision during critical moments. She portrays the emotional toll of mundane existence and the profound loneliness that can lurk behind closed doors. Yet, through her despair, she finds resilience, a testament to the strength found in moments of emotional overload. Her advice is clear: to find balance, one must look within and listen to the small, still voice that persists despite external turmoil.

Anne Melelita's verse also touches on themes of love and companionship in "My forever Man," where the entrance of a loving partner brings transformational energy into her life. This poem discusses the healing power of love and mutual acceptance, highlighting her journey of overcoming past traumas with the support of a partner who serves as both a confidant and a catalyst for change.

"Safety Boundaries" ventures into the concept of personal safety and boundaries. Anne Melelita contemplates the often confusing line between feeling safe and being truly safe, urging readers to establish and respect their boundaries as a crucial aspect of self-care and personal integrity.

The collection concludes with "Peace and Love," a reflective piece on identity and purpose. Here, Anne Melelita presents herself not just as a poet, but as a mother, a lover, a wife, and a friend. She discusses the ongoing challenge of picking up the pieces of her past to forge a clear path forward, emphasizing her role as a guide not only for her children and others but for herself first and foremost.

Anne Melelita Brown's poems are more than words on a page; they are a heartfelt invitation to journey alongside her through the complexities of life and the pursuit of authenticity and peace. Her work resonates with anyone who seeks to understand themselves and the world around them, making her collection a beacon of hope and a testament to the power of self-reflection and spiritual growth.

I am Okay Today

Today I'm in a place within
That I am okay
Feelings and emotions are within balance.
I am in a place that is stable.
As I sit at my solid table
I am able to focus on the moment.
and know I have done well
bouncing with energy and vesting
I am able to focus for now; I am calm.
No more harmful words from oneself.
Backtracking for focus, I was able to embrace
In my past, I had to reference individual
situations that have conditioned me today
knowing that change occurs almost every day
I say, whether the change is welcome or not.
One still has to work with what tools one has.
so at this moment in ones life
I find myself easy and breezy.
I am okay.
Love and Peace.

Sound of Truth

One, two, three.
Flee from change.
To realize is inevitable.
running most one's life
fight or flight
I found oneself lighting
69 times one has moved homes
and not to mention the men
when I came to wake one day
I found myself listening to the sound.
of truth, wisdom, consistency, & positiveness
I felt no more lifelessness.
I finally get it.
fight or flight
I found oneself fighting.
fighting to be me
No more fleeing.
because I can now see
one, two, three
I no longer flee.

Waiting Game

Each door that opens eventually closes.
This is how I deal with the past issues.
Past issues will eventually be haunts.
Letting go is the hardest.
"That I know."
Events that happened
still prods at my being
my spirit and psyche, soul still
unable to be free. and I'm unable to see
Confidence has gone.
judgments & lost
Belonging is a find.
and one's mind seems jumbled.
The constant fight one has within
inhibits one to moving forward
Frightened, that the Anne that is
will no longer be,
All I want is to be set free.
but still within one feels sadness
grief, loss, and fear
one's mask one wears
Is someone in a tiresome battle?

ECHOES OF THE SOUL

With each door that opens,
One, two, or three will close.
Waiting game still.

Christopher

You opened my vision.
When my eyes were closed
You jumped at me.
I jumped back.
You saw me.
I saw through you.
So I took that step forward towards you.
Something that I thought I wouldn't do
It was your inviting energy that welcomed mine.
I took matters to the next step.
for someone who was oblivious to your energy
I'm so enjoying your company.
We engaged with each other's consent.
Saying that I only wanted you to be casual
The days and the weeks went past.
Unknown to me, you became a permanent fix in my life.
This feels alright, I said; you welcomed me with your all.
Words really don't say what I am feeling.
You have made many of my wishes come true, yes you
To fight with what I am feeling for you
can remain as only being exciting, anew
and not frightening

You are like no other individual I've met.
A statement that has enticed my every whim
I've fallen in love with him.
Yes, you, my sweet prince,
I want to grow with you.
Let's show each other the true,
Meaning of true love
Together we will support each other's needs.
Together we will plant our seeds.
Together we take each other's hand.
Lead one another,
on our journey of love
All I know at this time is I'm liking how you make me feel.
I'm happy, excited, oversexed, and calm.
When with you and not with you
You have my heart,
You have me, myself, and I.
I'm yours forever, amen.
Love and Peace

Discovery

I feel as unstable as I have ever felt.
I feel like a bird, free.
I feel like I can conquer all.
I feel like I've set myself free.
found the true me
Now all I have to do is
find my abode
connecting with every emotion feeling within
learning how I can adapt
learning how to survive all over these years
has finally been somewhat sorted
I know now that my life has been an exceptional one.
and what has happened for me and my
past molds me for the future,
I say bring it on.
even though I'm feeling in control at present
I still understand that the journey
Self-discovery is unfolding accordingly.
to help adapt.
So I will endure life's uncertainties and accept ungrateful situations.
with an open mind.
I am grateful for what has happened.

or hasn't,
as my life has been definitely full of adventures
and more to come
so my attitude towards myself and
the way my life is at present
has to be accepted
and allow the journey to self-discovery
to continue.
Life has new meanings to me.
Love and Peace

Uncertainy

There are certain moments in time
that stay with one forever
One day at a time is how I live.
It gives one focus for the moment.
It allows one to be able and stable.
just like a very solid table
One's life has certainly been a challenge.
One can say I managed.
I know that I can be a nightmare
a scary movie too, and a thriller novel
But mostly I'm just living day by day and practicing with laughter
and humor.
And today starts anew again.
So to live with mental illness every day
and have it labeled various names
is something I really haven't fully come to terms with.
Please don't harbor your insecurities for our future.
Over the years I have gone from therapy to therapy to therapy.
Many crossed my path.
Group sessions,
I was taught to control what hindered within.
I was equipped to use the tools given to me.

I began to see that I could be free, free from the past burdens. Warning signs become a lot more coherent.

My Forever Man

In my heart there lay a wish.
That my prince charming would find me
a dream that belongs to a child
became an adult's wish come true
I have my prince charming.
well worth my lifetime of wait.
He is a man from my past.
The last time I looked, he still lived across the road.
For 5 years, he had his own family life.
Then that came to an end.
So did my relationship.
We both had time to self-discover.
Then you acknowledged me.
I feel weak in my knees.
Wow, wow, wow.
Within three days, we fell in love.
Wow, wow, wow.
we both admit that falling in love
with each other is welcoming wholeheartedly
So we will embrace our unity.
And finally one day we all become one.

ECHOES OF THE SOUL

One Wish

Alone no more is what I wished for.
I wished you in my life.
when I was only thirteen
You see, I was named Cinderella.
and when I was dreaming
I would wish for my prince charming.
to come and rescue me
Alas, he didn't come.
but I knew someday
He would lay his head.
with me, on my pillow
hold me and say
I am your prince, and you are my princess.
It's okay; you're safe.
because your prince will be there forever.
So through one's life, the search still continued.
Within all my relationships I had, I did move on.
Unfortunately, no prince.
I knew one day we would meet.
Love and Peace

My Man

It's time to embark on another adventure.
something that cannot be a hindrance anymore
I must soar and soar.
Allow myself to adventure to the higher level.
and know that the truth has always been there
and that is what I hold, my key to unlock my destiny.
It's me that is holding myself back.
It's always been me. with whom I battle.
It's always been me. unstable I was, and now that I see the truth finally
I am now able to take that first step.
That step is allowing my own judgment to matter so.
I need to be apart from my kind.
and enhance my very own attributes and qualities that have always been in me.
But was unsure how to use these tools.
Throughout my life's journey,
I have come to know that at the end of the day
It is I that has to come to terms with my lifetime of challenges.
I've accepted that what happened to me in my past only molds me into who I am today.
and I can only know that I have my future ahead of me

and that I will indeed succeed.
So I will open my soul and my heart and allow the white light to
really guide me.
So my adventure that I'm now on
is self-discovery.
And I found it excitingly closer.
closer to a part of my emotions and feelings.
Allow the best judge to take over me!
So the question that has been prodding me is
so what do I want, and is what I'm doing getting me it?
I say yes.
Love and peace.

Embark on Another Adventure

Each door that opens eventually closes.
This is how I deal with the past issues.
Past issues will eventually be haunts.
Letting go is the hardest.
"That I know."
Events that happened
still prods at my being
my spirit and psyche, soul still
unable to be free. and I'm unable to see
Confidence has gone.
judgments & lost
Belonging is a find.
and one's mind seems jumbled.
The constant fight one has within
inhibits one to moving forward
Frightened, that the Anne that is
will no longer be,
All I want is to be set free.
but still within one feels sadness
grief, loss, and fear
one's mask one wears
Is someone in a tiresome battle?

ANNE MELELITA BROWN

With each door that opens,
One, two, or three will close.
Waiting game still.

Tears That Fall Suddenly

As I sit and ponder about my past
I can honestly say, "Well done to me!"
as I faced challenging issues
Yes, tears did fall, and I used tissues.
but with the tools that I learned and practiced and
With the support of all, I gently managed my calls.
I can say, "Well done to me."
Stable for the moment is good enough for me.
As I wake every morning, tired.
I know that today is a new day.
the way to make your day a good day
Stay positive and open to receive.
So if the wind blows hard and you fall
and the rain pounds heavy,
No sunshine for days; that's okay.
Remember that whatever state your mind is in
The sun always shines and finds that
the rainbow that one searches for,
So don't ignore feelings and emotions that jump.
One is always focused; it's just that
gray clouds
does get in the way and stays as long as one wants

ANNE MELELITA BROWN

So if your tears fall suddenly
Not to worry, for crying is not a trying time.
It's a way to let go and to know.
I have achieved a lot and got a lot.
with my beliefs and knowledge, support
I am capable of achieving my desired goals.
knowing that the past is the past
I can at least say one year is gone, another to come.
Well done to me.
love and light

A Moment Feeling

Uncertainty clouds my thought
At a moment that vision is needed
As my future seems afar,
eager to move ahead
My life seems mundane and unfulfilled
my energy has no life
My daunting spirit traps me to focus clearly
Today I have no smile and the bounce
I had yesterday has gone
Behind closed doors ones life seems lonely
With a prodding feeling of hopelessness and despondency
Emotional overload
Eyes are feeling heavy
Tears don't stop
Need to find the strength to end the pain that turns
Knowing that this is only a moment and it will pass
I still find that ones belief is gone
A moment can be as long or short
Depends on the issue at hand
So if one knows how to tell the signs before
Emotional overload
Use it as this will make any situation a lot clearer

ANNE MELELITA BROWN

and one will feel a lot calmer
To find the balance for the outside
Look within
So if one's moment feeling gets somewhat clouded
And no one's voices on the outside is helping
Remember that the little voice within is always available

Resolving Past Issues

Compel my thoughts every day.
Facing one's fears and trying hard to hold back the tears
Don't give up, Don't give up. Don't give up.
Is all I hear, in my head, feeling somewhat dead?
An emptiness still prods at me.
Having what I have dreamt about
Until the most loving man I have ever known
Materialized into my life
sharing and communicating our thoughts
We share what is
What can be
And what will be
With our changes, we accept each other.
Our challenges
Knowing that my issues from past experiences still hinder
My thoughts and being
You challenge me with acceptance.
You support and understand me with my fears.
Only you wipe my tears.
I am on the path to resolving past haunts.
And pleased that you are by my side.
Facing past, now, and future concerns with you

ANNE MELELITA BROWN

Makes my healing process twice as fast.
And I can leave the past haunts.
With a proud smile and a knowing of another completion
One door shuts and another opens.
And you are my key.
Love and Peace

Safety Boundaries

Safety pulls within me, tugging at my inner questions.
Questions that confuse my thoughts
Feeling safe and being safe—that question continuously hounds me.
I should know the answer; the question has always been in me.
Is one safe with oneself, or is one using tools of past events?
So one can determine one's boundaries when the safety issues arise.
It arises in my thoughts continuously and physically.
Where do one's boundaries start and end?
To enable one to compromise with oneself, where do one's boundaries lie?
So for one to acknowledge this, one has to call upon the strength within.
if one is unaware of an issue that does not need boundaries,
Acknowledge this and think.
One has to focus and welcome this newfound outlet into one's life.
Boundaries will always be an issue, as day-to-day has many challenges.
Boundaries are not what we are but what we have become because of it.
For the knowledge of how to act and not to act lies always within; why does one procrastinate knowing that the intentions are tugging within?

Why is one unable to make a decision at a time when one's expectations are so defined?
that one cannot attain the desire, the pull within.
The head is saying yes.
The heart is saying no.
Boundaries are what is needed.
Balancing out situations that need one's utmost undivided attention.
So keep up the boundaries.
Always stay true to yourself.
Respect oneself and others.
Use your boundaries, not to hurt, but to be alert.
So procrastinate no more.
as one acknowledges faults that need to be explored.
Love and Peace

Who am I?

I am a mother.
I've been a lover.
I've been a wife.
And I've been a friend to many as the years have passed all so fast.
I'm left with shattered pieces of my past.
Pieces in which I have to mend
And try not to go around the bend.
As I'm working without identity
I ask my questions once more.
Who am I?
Why am I here?
Am I a woman with a lot of integrity?
I'm a woman that doesn't judge.
I am a woman with needs.
I'm a woman that definitely intrigues
My directions have once more clouded my thoughts.
I am aware of this.
I can trust in the way and reign my faith.
Pick up the pieces, and the puzzles of life will be clearer.
Who am I?
I am me.
someone special that rings laughter and hope into others lives

and also my own
I am here to be all that I can.
And to guide my children and others that cross my path,
But most of all, I am here to guide myself first.
So my past tissues may have a profound experience of all the future
I will do the best one can.
And always remember, life will always have its next challenges, but
I will always try to be me.
Love and Peace

The Beach

As i sit in the still of night
I look up to the stars above
I close my eyes, them reopen them
I saw three shooting stars
Breath taken by surprise
Once more close my eyes
and made my 3 wishes. . .
The night so peaceful, not a sound to be heard
only the waves that emerge onto the sand
The oceans so calm
I feel so at ease, and very pleased
my mind at rest
My spirit is blessed
my soul leaps
my heart beeps
I saw 3 falling stars.

Ray of Sunshine

You are my ray of sunshine.
You have awoken my soul and sprite.
You have astounded my thoughts.
You have captured my attention.
Something I never thought possibly would ever happen
So knowing you has been a pleasure.
My ray of sunshine
Butterflies flutter around in my tummy.
A sensual feeling overwhelms me.
This is how it feels when I think about you.
Feelings that confuse me
Are your words true?
Are your intentions honorable?
Or are my thoughts and actions too spontaneous?
Nevertheless
I will trust in my feelings.
Something that is needed
Your nature is so inviting.
Your appearance is beautiful.
Your knowledge is so gifted.
Your sense of humor, I can definitely say, makes me laugh.
Your presence grounds me.

Your kisses are so gentle.
Your body so close to mine sends chills up and down my spine.
Your smile is so true.
Your eyes are so intense that I shy away when I look at you.
So again I say you have awoken my soul and spirit.
You have astounded my thoughts.
A feeling of calm comes over me.
Our connection seems unreal.
Our energy is so amazing.
So let's just enjoy each other.
Take it day by day.
And if we were meant to be, it will be.
When I look at you, I see the sunshine.
Sunshine upon me
My ray of sunshine
Peace and Love

Moving Forward

To move forward is a big step.
Change should be a good thing.
So then why does it frighten us so?
when we are reluctant to have change in our lives?
Afraid of what the consequences will be from past experiences
You must want change with all your heart.
Trust in your intuition.
and you will find the way
Trust in yourself.
Trust in your heart, not your head.
Then only you can make your decision.
and that decision you have chosen
is to make the change for oneself
So, to stand new next time, you must leave the old ways behind.
and trust in the way
So, to change one's life, you must want to.
And to want it, you must go to get it.
So, don't be afraid.
Spread your wings; you will know.
that in life you will grow
as you allow that
So, pat yourself on the back.

ECHOES OF THE SOUL

because the change you will make
will be a positive one
Always remember you are not alone.
So, take the change.
head held high
to know that you have been here before
You can move forward.
Peace and love.

Strength

A feeling of despondency submits to me.
A feeling of anxiousness overwhelms me.
A feeling of emotional overload.
A feeling of depleted energy exhausts.
A feeling of no self-worth, no confidence.
Eyes are feeling heavy; tears won't stop.
Thoughts are so much unfocused.
Then I asked myself, what is it that needs to be seen?
What is happening to me? What's going on in my head?
What is happening within me?
How do I feel at this moment? What is my breathing doing?
These questions override my negative thoughts.
Strength is what is required for this moment.
As I reach deep within, my strength comes once again.
At a time, one feels extreme uncontrollable thoughts.
So, I calm one's destructive thoughts.
with kind words of support
my own kind words
Peace and love.

ECHOES OF THE SOUL

The Fight for Love

What is the abundance of love?
Is one able to comply with my answers in which one does not know?
one perspective at a time when one wants to be loved
may seem all mixed up
sorrow in which one has always mends in love, or does it
One strides through one's life to find purpose.
to find the love one longs for
But instead the hurt gets stronger.
and the purpose to find love
flies away just like a dove
Again, one is left with the nagging questions.
and the empty feeling of longing
Why can't I find true love?
Lonely no more is all I wish for.
Can one word be heard above?
That is the question that no one longs to know.
But really, can they hear my cries above?
as I close my eyes and open them to
Uncertainties in my day ask my questions again.
Where is love, and where can I find it?
How long can one wait?

when one knows there is no longer any laughter
and loneliness compels one's being
Men come and go; still not true love.
Nevertheless, one will continue to search for one's true love.

Hurtful Words

Why do words hurt one so?
Knowing that one should let them bounce
knowing what has been said
What if hurtful words come from a loved one?
hurtful words that pierce one's inner being
knowing that judgment day has come again
But still, the words hurt one deep.
Do they really know me?
Do they know who I am?
Do they only see what they want?
Do they really hear my words?
Or do I portray myself in a way that I am talked about?
I hear the whispers behind me.
Nevertheless, I am who I am, and I have feelings.
dealing with issues and situations The best ones can
But do they really know me?
My appearance on the outside is stable and carefree.
And on the inside, I'm singing the blues.
Therefore, no one really knows who I am.
So, every negative word I hear
I will accept it gracefully, knowing that one should let them bounce.

So, if hurtful words cross your path,
Allow your dignity and wisdom. Create something positive from
something negative.
In a time that is needed
So, try and let those hurtful words lie.
Also remember they are only words.
and they can't hurt you
unless you let them.
Peace and love.

Easiest Way Out

I am unable to remain still.
When the tough gets going, the going gets rough.
Throughout my life, I ran away from my fears.
instead of staying to face them
I seem to jump on the first available flight.
At the time, it seemed the easiest way out.
my endeavors that I have experienced
Seem to hinder my capabilities of acceptance.
So, I retreat, then run.
run as far away as possible
thinking that the issues have been left behind
But instead it comes creeping up, tapping on my shoulder.
Saying hello, there, you forgot me.
So, an issue that should have been dealt with
Prior to the running, it is now twice as troublesome to me.
I should have reflected on the situation prior to running away.
At the end of the day, I should have stayed put.
Now things are twice as hard.
I am now in my thirties and have moved around so many times.
I have come to realize that most of my life
I have run and run and run.
No more running.

So, I stay put this time and fix what is broken.
face my fears that have constricted me
Over the years, I have been in flight mode.
Today I am in fight mode.
So, I manage my life's ups and downs.
the best way I can
Not to run away, sort it out.
So I stayed here for 5 years.
Then it's time for me to move again.
Knowing that for me to move again, this time I am not running
Instead, circumstances have allowed me to leave gracefully.
Something I am not used to.
So, I embrace my surroundings with happiness.
and says to me
It doesn't take courage to run away.
It takes courage to stay.

Mother

Words spoken but not heard
Why is it that you don't hear me?
Why is it that you don't see me?
Why is it that you don't speak kindly?
words to me
You see me as you wanted to.
judging me to the extreme
not acknowledging me as an individual
Instead, you would rather label me.
Kind words for me are seeing that, won't happen.
As my past events have some downfalls,
as my life is not how you wish it for me
But you have to accept that I coped the best way I could.
Acknowledging the failures has been in my past.
But, Mother, what is it you can't tell me?
What is it that you only see?
What is it that disappoints you about me?
It hurts me so.
to know that my mother,
is only able to judge me,
Please hear my words and speak to me.
with gentle words.

and know that I love you.
And thank you for my life.
But one problem is still not solved.
Love and Peace

Twin Flame

One's lifetime partner
In a way, I would acknowledge him to be
a connection that is so deep
with a sense of mystery that constrains my thoughts
not knowing, just dissipation, anticipation
Intrigued with self-pleasure
words that capture my thoughts
Intelligence with a hint of skepticism
someone I could admire and be inspired by
a passion for zest
stability within oneself and one's surroundings
ground so deep that when you speak,
the words of wisdom
You should speak of truth and life experience.
also understand each other's need for space
sharing with each other all we know and hold dear
Your energy has to be vibrant.
Your spirit has to be free and in tune.
Your aura should be inviting.
Your mind has to be overrated.
My twin flame is what I'm in search of.
your love for music, in which contains the key

the key to harmony of emotions that ran free
as the essence of sexual attraction already prods at me
something that we both, breathtakingly, admit
that when we make love, we both are able to feel free
Our hearts should intertwine with a love that is combined.
Our actions should have no limits.
I deserve this man, viewed from my desires.
and a man that makes me laugh
and compels me, in every way.
Love and peace.

Ones Needs

I am a woman with strength.
a woman who has survived once again and again and again
the cruelty of being responsible in one's life
can be extremely exhausting
I am a woman of excellence.
My appearance is very curvaceous.
just like my outlook on life
I have a heart that needs to beat.
And I have a man that makes me leap.
I need love, in which I can give back.
not lust that yearns
I need to be hugged, a very strong hug.
that will make me feel safe and all nice and snug
I need to feel safe.
safe in myself and safe with you
I need conversations, not words that bounce.
I need someone that will listen.
Listen to my words, my needs.
Most of all, listen to me.
Love and Peace

Who Are You

Where are you, and who are you?
I find myself asking every day.
anxious for you to enter my life
my soulmate I'm in search of
You will have to be a man with a heart.
a man that has a spirit
a man with hopes and dreams and,
a man that loves pleasure
Do you stand so tall?
With a smile, that is true.
eyes that are intense and shine like the stars in the sky
Integrity has to be within.
Are you stable within yourself and with your surroundings?
Can you handle any situation on your own?
Are you willing to share your decisions and problems?
just to share yourself with me
Where are you? I ask myself
Can you hear my calls?
Are you near or far?
When will I know?
So in the meantime? I will visualize your appearance every day.
So until we meet

ANNE MELELITA BROWN

Patience is required.
so for now and later
I'll just wait.
Because if you are meant to be, you will be.
So where are you, and who are you?
Love and Peace

Marriage to You

I didn't need the hurt.
I didn't need the pain.
I didn't need someone like you.
I've been asking myself, what went wrong?
between me and you
It has taken many years of soul searching to come to some contentment.
Am I who I am, and that I had lost while with you?
memories of our marriage together,
always has me asking, why? What went wrong?
I now can see a man that has no true
a man that has no virtues
I needed your respect, not your neglect.
I feel I was nothing in your eyes.
I trusted you with my life.
and I found I always tried ending it in strife.
knowing you for so long
You wouldn't think I would know you inside and out.
Unfortunately, we both fall with that.
but our time together was not wanted.
as we have three beautiful boys, and I have no regrets
We really have nothing in common.

ANNE MELELITA BROWN

I have lived and lied for many years.
habits, habits, habits—that's what you are.
I want to share so much of me, but you really didn't care.
lacking self-esteem, lacking confidence, just lacking in my spirit
I was not happy in our marriage.
So I will look at our marriage in a positive light.
and let's stop the fights.
as we are both adults and have separate lives now
You broke my heart many times over.
Then that wasn't enough; you broke my spirit and shattered my pride.
Why, I ask? Did you hurt me so?
I trusted you and gave you so much.
I saw you as an individual that needs me.
I loved you but wasn't in love with you.
I still love you, but in a way that I would love a tree.
The marriages we had are now memories.
the positive things about being married to you,
was the children and finding myself
So thank you for who I am today.
because without your experiences together, I would not have
Knowing what I do know now.
Wishing you the best, and may you find it in your heart.
to stand still and find yourself, your true self.
God bless, and I wish you well.
Love and Peace

Ones Confidence

One is surrounded by beauty.
Taking a breath in, exhaling, and sighing with relief
Thank you for what one has in one's life.
Thank you for what I now know and have known.
Thank you for the guidance and the beliefs I have.
Thank you for my life.
I am more aware.
I am more exhilarated with a hint of diversity.
So believe in oneself, that to achieve one's goals, dreams
relates to the state of mind that one has
So positive reactions are needed.
at a time when all that seems to be doing is negative thinking
stand still, stand still, stand still
One has to stand still, to breathe, to move forward.
Within time, one can focus on any issue with no hesitation.
comfort oneself with kind words of wisdom
comfort oneself with knowing that everything will be okay
comfort oneself with knowing positive friends
comfort oneself with one's needs
realize that one has to be loved by the self
Encouragement and self take form from the depth of the soul.
Enable your spirit, mind, and soul to be balanced and focused.

ANNE MELELITA BROWN

Take a breath in and exhale, sighing with relief.
I have done it once again.
Love and peace.

Through My Eyes

One is molded as a child, with the help of adults.
As ones still very young, one's intelligence has not yet enabled us to focus on oneself.
So any guidance through growing up has come from parents, teachers, friends, and even a stranger.
once one is old enough to adventure outside
out in a world that contains uncertainties,
To do this is very frightening and exhilarating.
To those that have and will do so, I have this to say:
Perseverance is what it takes.
to make a life, not so you will retreat
but a life that you will defeat
hold one's head high with pride
Feel the fear and do it anyway.
Remember that one has control of one's life.
To maintain one's sanity can be very exhausting.
Try to adapt to the surroundings and issues the way one knows.
Don't push oneself to the limit, or one will find oneself submitting down.
if one is feeling overwhelmed, in which tears do fall silent
fall with an uncontrollable outburst
Tears that once were silent can now be heard.

ANNE MELELITA BROWN

words that dare not pass one's lips
Now leap out with satisfaction.
You see, I have observed this through one's eyes.
To be heard, one has to talk.
if one is feeling confused and scared
Just believe that things will get better.
even if it is just for a short time
So if time out is needed, do so.
Listen to the little voice within.
It's okay to feel like this.
Life is our playground.
lots of roller coasters and many merry-go-rounds
Just proceed the best way one can.
Peace and love.

Life's Uncertainties

Do you ever wonder why we are here?
To be able to determine our life purpose
Is it a race of survival, or is it just destiny?
Or is it just a waste of your precious time?
What is it that one is to think when there is no way you are able to move ahead?
What is life, and what's its purpose?
being misled down a path of uncertainty
Again, what is one to think?
Think of all the mistakes or lessons one has endured.
only to trade one thought with a look of taunt
trying to maintain alert and aware behavior
or get knocked down again and again
picking up oneself and holding your head higher than before
As the seasons change, so do we.
As the rain falls, so do our tears and fears.
As we grow, so does nature and everyone around us.
as we listen to the words from above
one's eyes close, to rest once more
I open my eyes wide and say
Good morning to everyone.
Today is another day of uncertainties.

ANNE MELELITA BROWN

So the way to survive is to take it day by day.
Life can be a challenge.
among a lot of things
When we are all single, we are lonely.
when we feel down and stressed
Just remember that asking for help is always the best.
as we have all had our share of uncertainties
So our life's purpose is to trod along, fully alert.
Life is beautiful.
nature is a gift
humans with gratitude
astonishing theories from our ancestors era
so to maintain balance in one's life
remain sincere
and if one has not found one's life purpose
Keep searching, and you will find one.
Peace and Love

Better Within

A constant battle goes on inside my head.
Stillness doesn't happen very often…
I find myself up and down…
most of the time,time,time lying the ground
Why is it that cannot contain my actions???
Hurting oneself is the easy way out…
Why is it that am unable to control
my momentary feeling of wanting to die
Why is it that I am unable to control the urge to take one'ss life??
knowing that it is not right
Negative energy andand negative words overrule me..
but knowing that I am in a a constant battle with myself.
The positive me submits and lets the negative me completely take
over.
The pain I feel is so intense.
the hurt that races throughout my body
is a constant reminder of past issues
Tears that fall, fall heavy.
unable to focus, unable to hear
thoughts racing through me,
thoughts that don't even belong to me, I create
Can I ever find stillness?

ANNE MELELITA BROWN

Can I ever obtain peace within one's thoughts?
Or will the constant battle within allow one to find the way?
to move highs and lows
I would like to stop the pain.
Stop the hurt, stop the fears, and
most of all to stop me from hurting myself again
and for my tears to stop.
Love and peace.

Guiding Hand

One cannot disguise what one feels inside for too long.
emotions within, always spin
An uncomfortable urge overwhelms me.
The pounding of my heart starts to beat very fast.
Thoughts become too much.
Tears fall from my eyes.
All I want is to be safe.
All I want is to feel the love, the love from within.
All I want is stability within me.
will one keep experiencing
Tears fall from my eyes.
When do the tears stop? That is one finds saying most of the time.
What is it that remains unforeseen?
Can I rid myself of the pain and anger that dwells deep within?
or will one keep spinning and not find an end?
as I once again ask for direction
I am pointed into your guidance.
with a sigh of relief
I am able to trust in your presence and your words.
I know you are in my life, as I allowed it.
The choice I have made is one that remains to excel.
You have shown me ways of adapting.

ANNE MELELITA BROWN

You have listened to my words I speak.
I find that you are able to take a situation that troubles me.
You mold it in a way I can understand.
Thoughts that I thought not possible are now planted in my mind.
To me, you're my guiding hand.
You will free me from my past.
I am tired of living in fear.
So therefore, I will stay.
until the way becomes clear
Thank you for your guiding hand.
Love and peace.

Today Is Another Day

Today I am now with friends.
as we speak to each other
We all share our stories.
with a listening ear
just supportive words of encouragement
Yesterday has gone, tomorrow has come.
ding dong ding dong
I don't belong, and loneliness at
Feelings we all have expressed at some time.
searches for one's purpose in life.
There is not one purpose.
There are multiple purposes.

Look Within

Look within to find the answers, or not.
answers to questions and what we search for
Sometimes one has to let the situation
mould one's moment of why.
Trying to make sense of something that is trusting one
One needs to have an ego of letting it be.
one will see that within hours, days, and weeks
the answer that one seeks.
will be relevant to one's purpose

For So Long

For so long, I've been fighting this constant battle.
between myself and me.
Why, I ask. Why does this happen to me?
Why am I so unkind to myself?
Why do I want to hurt me?
Why don't the tears stop?
and the constant battle within shall continue.
Why am I unable to balance with the now, past?
and to come
Why is it that when I feel that finally things are going ok?
I seem to engage in self-doubt and self-pity. Oh, oh, I.
I want to free myself from my own shackles.
Cut the tie that bounds me to whatever holds me back.
So will my constant battle, within, surrender.
Allow me to find solutions for all that hinders me.
Can I find the stableness that prods at me daily?
Can I emerge into the New or
Am I going to continue with this constant battle?

Would Like To Happen

Would like to happen
would not like to happen
I find myself in a black hole.
Uncontrollable urges submerge.
Feelings of hopelessness start to arise.
unable to maintain calmness
I find myself with the past.
spinning around my head.
I need kind words of support.
not words that pierce like a dagger.
but words that are strong and firm
I have never wished it on anyone.
unless I am provoked
But I am who I am.
I am a very unique individual.
who has qualities that embrace all.
I will always remain a free spirit.
but for me to remain still within me
I have to find home.
and that I have not attained just you
I believe that I have a path that branches in every direction.
and for me to find that stableness I have

ECHOES OF THE SOUL

to go through what I do.

Anne Melelita is Very Happy

Anne Melelita is very happy.
at this moment in time
lime green, looks good
I devised it myself.
combed my hair
I stare in the mirror.
one last touch
I put a colorful
flower in my hair
Then I start my day.
I say to myself
Let's go with the flow.
only to know that
Anne Melelita is very happy.
with her life today
all because of you

Silent Whispers

I'm not crazy.
I'm just a little unbalanced.
I know that others talk about me.
I can hear their whispers.
whispers that come right back to me
just because one can be somewhat different
doesn't mean that one is mental and other harsh words
Criticism does not help one's self-esteem.
especially when they come from ones that you trust and love.
Silent whispers can be heard.
Why is it that the support that is needed from those who don't give?
but with it comes that back chat
Okay, I know that my life hasn't been perfect, but whose has?
I find myself justifying to others,
Why am I where I am?
but for me to judge me
knowing that if they needed support
I'll be there with no qualms.
But really, do they have to be so crucial?
Do they need to throw my past at me?
Can't they see that I know my journey is somewhat unusual?
in the eyes of pretentious individuals

Peace and Love

Why me?
Why my life?
Why is it that I'm the unstable one?
Why is it that my life has been very eventful?
just want peace within totally
a home to call my own
Can this be attended?
I cannot see.
I just want to find my home base.
and while I don't know my direction
I have to stay where I know will be safe.
and that's with my family.
I've found over my life I have found living
with them has been very selfish for all
All I want is a home to call my own.
to know that I will be grounded and stable.
So this wish has been a dream.

Reflection and an Invitation

In the closing pages of Anne Melelita Brown's poetry collection, we find a resonant conclusion that serves both as a reflection and an invitation. Through her intimate verses, Anne has shared a deeply personal journey marked by struggle, growth, and eventual peace. Her poetry does not shy away from the complexities of the human condition; instead, it embraces them, crafting a narrative that intertwines the trials of life with the beauty of overcoming.

As readers, we are invited to find pieces of ourselves within her stories—to recognize our own fears, hopes, and revelations within her words. Anne's poetry acts as a mirror, reflecting our own lives back at us, encouraging us to confront our realities with the same courage she has shown. Her final poems underscore a powerful message of resilience and self-acceptance, urging us to continue on our paths with determination and self-compassion.

Anne's work culminates in a celebration of the self and an acknowledgment of the power within each of us to shape our destinies. She reminds us that while life is fraught with challenges, it is also filled with moments of profound joy and fulfillment. By guiding herself and her readers toward understanding and acceptance, Anne's poems offer a soothing balm for the soul, suggesting that peace comes not from perfection but from embracing the entirety of our experiences.

This collection closes on a note of hopeful continuity, suggesting that the journey of self-discovery and spiritual connection is ongoing. Anne leaves us with the understanding that every end is simply a new beginning, and each of us has the strength to carry forward, to write our own stories with courage and love. As we turn the final page, we are not at the end but at a threshold, poised to take the next steps on our own transformative journeys, inspired by the wisdom and beauty of Anne M. Brown's poetic explorations.

Meet Anne Melelita

Anne Melelita Brown is a beacon of kindness and creativity hailing from the lush landscapes of New Zealand. As a poet, Anne Melelita crafts verses that resonate with warmth and depth, reflecting her gentle spirit and loving nature. A devoted mother to five wonderful children, she embodies the virtues of patience and care, always willing to lend a helping hand to those around her. When she's not weaving words into poetry, Anne Melelita can be found in the joyful company of her energetic border collie, Ash, exploring the scenic beauty of her homeland. Her work not only captures the essence of her experiences but also serves as an inspiration for her readers to find beauty and kindness in their daily lives.

www.ingramcontent.com/pod-product-compliance
Lightning Source LLC
Chambersburg PA
CBHW051948160426
43198CB00013B/2352